EXPLORING CAREERS WITHOUT COLLEGE

VOCATIONAL CAREERS IN WELLNESS AND BEAUTY

by Cynthia Kennedy Henzel

BrightPoint Press

San Diego, CA

an imprint of ReferencePoint Press, Inc.
Printed in the United States

For more information, contact:
BrightPoint Press
PO Box 27779
San Diego, CA 92198
www.BrightPointPress.com

LIBRARY OF CONGRESS CATALOGING-IN-PUBLICATION DATA

Name: Henzel, Cynthia Kennedy, author.
Title: Vocational careers in wellness and beauty / by Cynthia Kennedy Henzel.
Description: San Diego, CA: ReferencePoint Press, 2026 | Series: Exploring careers without college | Includes bibliographical references and index. | Audience: Grades 7–9
Identifiers: ISBN 9781678212780 (hardcover) | ISBN 9781678212797 (eBook)
The complete Library of Congress record is available at www.loc.gov.

CONTENTS

THE WELLNESS AND BEAUTY INDUSTRY AT A GLANCE

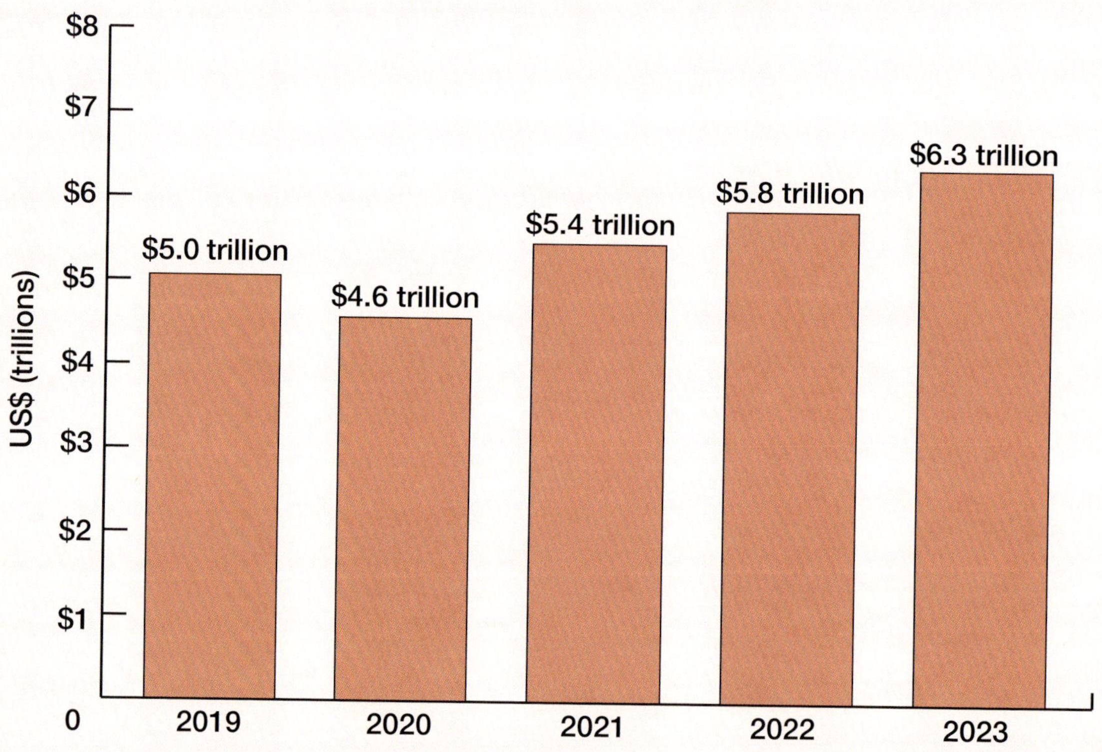

Source: "Wellness Economy Statistics & Facts," Global Wellness Institute, *n.d., https://globalwellnessinstitute.org.*

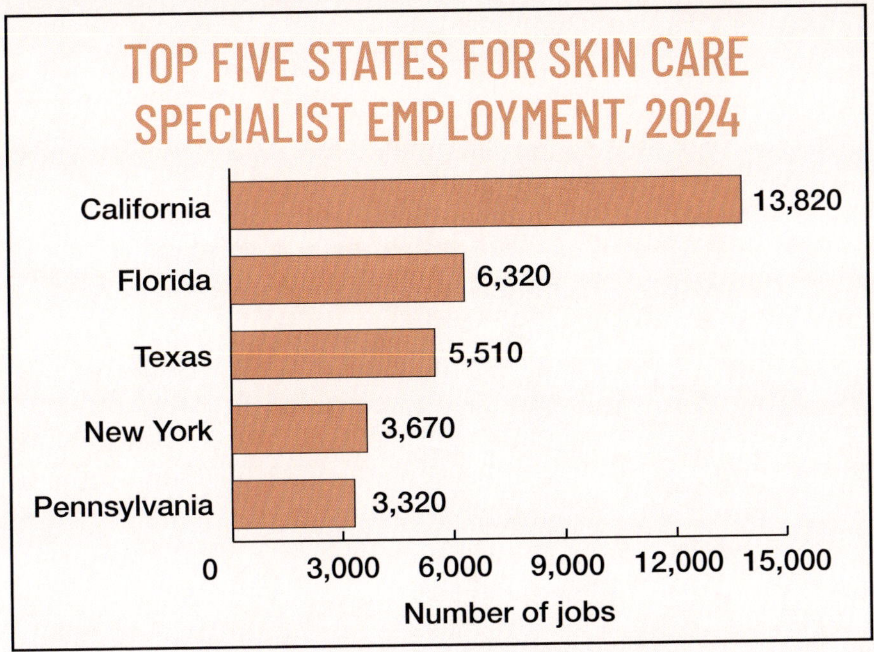

Source: "Occupational Employment and Wage Statistics Profiles: Skincare Specialists," US Bureau of Labor Statistics, *May 2024, https://data.bls.gov.*

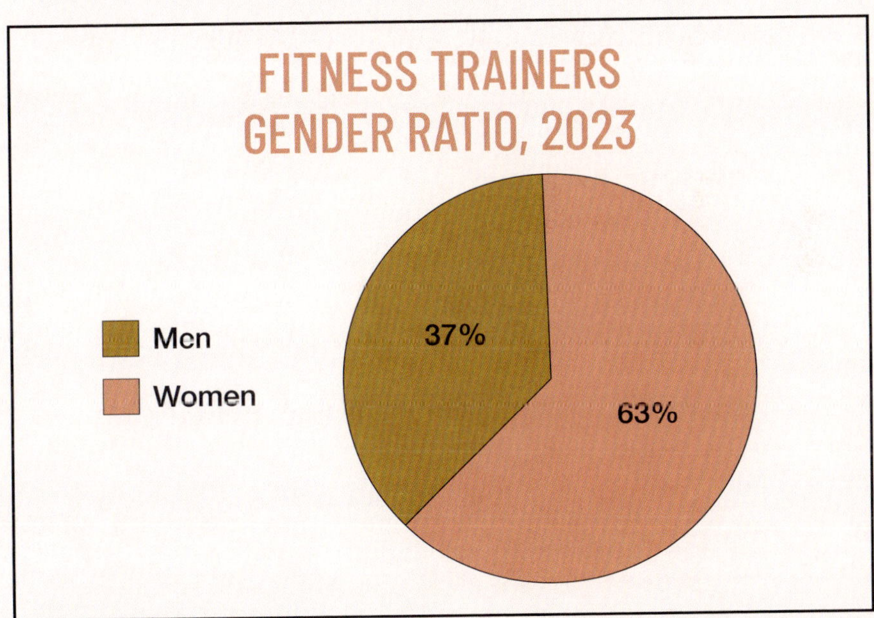

Source: "Exercise Trainers and Group Fitness Instructors," Data USA*, n.d., https://datausa.io.*

WHAT IS THE WELLNESS AND BEAUTY INDUSTRY?

As a kid, Rachel Henshaw knew she wanted to be a massage therapist. At first, she did not know everything a massage therapist did. But Henshaw liked science and **anatomy**. She also enjoyed solving problems. These included how to lower someone's pain or stress. She wanted to help people become healthier and happier.

Massage therapists can work in a variety of places, including spas, fitness centers, hospitals, and people's homes.

Creating a relaxing environment can help a person feel calmer and more comfortable during a massage.

Henshaw eventually found a massage therapy school she liked. The labs used **cadavers**. These helped her understand more about muscles. It was hard work. But she did well in school. Her first job was at a local health club.

Henshaw hoped to someday have her own office. But she knew she needed some experience. She worked with many clients.

She learned things that her anatomy courses did not teach.

One thing Henshaw learned was how to read body cues. A flinch meant pain. Slowed breathing showed relaxation. This told her when people were comfortable or uncomfortable. She listened to what people did or did not say. This helped her figure out how her clients felt. Henshaw learned how to work with people dealing with sadness or pain. And she discovered how great it was to help people feel better.

After 1 year, Henshaw's days were full of appointments. She worked on people who had different needs. And she worked on people from different backgrounds. Being a massage therapist was better than anything Henshaw had imagined as a kid.

THE BUSINESS OF FEELING GOOD

Careers in wellness focus on helping people feel better. Massage therapists and fitness trainers are some examples. Other services help clients follow healthy diets. Wellness workers help clients who are ill. They also help people recover from accidents. But wellness is not just about fixing problems. It is also about encouraging a healthy lifestyle.

Careers in beauty include services that help people look better. Some examples include hairstylists, skin care specialists, and nail care professionals. Other beauty services involve using makeup. The wellness and beauty industry keeps people feeling and looking their best.

Professionals in the wellness and beauty industry aim to help people feel their best both physically and mentally.

MASSAGE THERAPIST

Massage is a type of therapy. It uses touch to **manipulate** the soft tissues in the body. Muscles are soft tissues. So are tendons and ligaments. Tendons are tissues that attach muscles to bones. Ligaments connect bones. Massage can help relieve pain. It can relax tired or overworked muscles. Massage also helps muscles feel better after sports or injuries.

Massage therapists must have good communication skills so they know what areas of a client's body to focus on during a session.

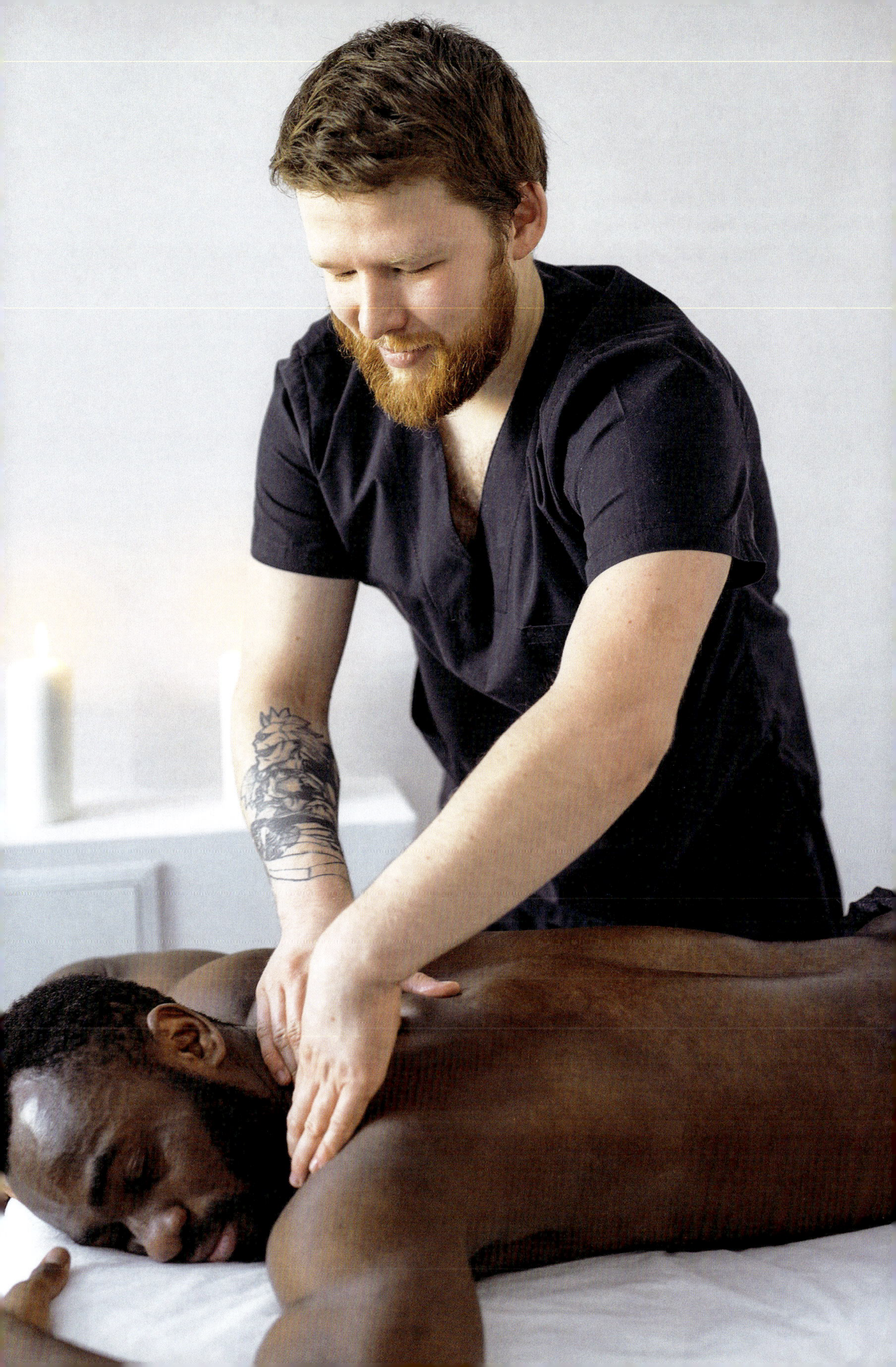

Massage can help relieve mental stress, too. It can lower some natural chemicals in the body. One is cortisol. This controls the body's reaction to stress. Massage therapists create a relaxing space for

Massage Therapist

Minimum Education: High school diploma, vocational school

Personal Qualities: Compassion, physical strength, communication skills

Certification and Licensing: Massage and Bodywork Licensing Examination, state licensing

Working Conditions: Massage therapists are often self-employed and work part-time. They stand for many hours and might use a lot of their strength during a massage.

Average Salary: $57,950 (2024)

Number of Jobs: 147,100 (2023)

Future Job Outlook: 18 percent growth expected between 2023 and 2033

their clients. They may use aromatherapy. Aromatherapy involves using scented oils on the skin. This helps relax clients. Therapists often play calming music. Many people use massage to improve their general health.

GETTING STARTED

Massage therapists need a high school diploma. They then attend a vocational program. These programs teach different massage techniques. They also provide hands-on training. This allows students to practice massage. Some programs are only a few weeks. Others may be 1 to 2 years.

After finishing their program, students take an exam. It is called the Massage and Bodywork Licensing Examination (MBLEx).

Knowing proper massage techniques and human anatomy helps therapists prevent injuries to themselves and clients.

MBLEx covers the physical parts of massage. And it covers principles and laws about working as a massage therapist. Most states also require therapists to get a license to work. Each state's requirements can be found through the American Massage Therapy Association (AMTA).

Many students continue their education by learning more types of massage.

Massage therapy has many specialties. The AMTA website lists more than 65 types. Swedish massage is the most common. Therapists use soft strokes and a light touch. This releases tense muscles. It also helps people relax.

Deep tissue massage is also common. Therapists apply hard pressure to release muscle tension. Deep tissue massage promotes injury **rehabilitation**. Sports therapists use deep tissue massage. It can help athletes recover from injuries. Sports therapists also use stretching. This increases flexibility. It also helps prevent future injury.

Another type of massage uses acupressure. These therapists apply pressure to specific points along the body.

These areas are called pressure points. Some people believe applying pressure to these areas can help manage depression and anxiety. Reflexology is another form of massage. This involves applying pressure to certain points only on people's hands and feet.

Massage therapists may use more than one technique. Cindy Williams is a

Fibromyalgia

Fibromyalgia is a condition that causes widespread muscle pain. Little is known about the condition. Experts believe it is likely passed down through families. It might also be related to extreme stress. Fibromyalgia has no cure. However, some research shows that massage can help ease the symptoms.

A hot stone massage involves placing heated, smooth stones along specific parts of a person's body. This helps relax muscles and reduce stress.

massage therapist. She says, "Every body is different, so my approach is always different." Williams says she tries new techniques to help clients. Or she may change the order of the techniques. If that does not work, she does research. This might include watching educational videos. Doing so helps her figure out how to solve a certain problem. Williams might also talk to another therapist. She can see what they know. “I never stop learning and growing,” Williams says.[1]

ON THE JOB

Therapists have a lot of flexibility in their jobs. About one-third of massage therapists are self-employed. Others work for personal care services. These include salons. Some work in doctor’s offices. Therapists often work part-time. Giving a massage takes a lot of strength. So many therapists do not work a full 8-hour day.

Massage therapists begin a session by talking with their client. They ask about a client’s symptoms. They make the client feel comfortable and safe. Therapists give clients a moment to remove their clothing.

Clients often cover themselves with a light blanket. Then they sit in a massage chair or lie on a table.

The therapist locates the painful or tense muscles in the body. They begin to manipulate the soft tissues. They might use their hands or fingers. The therapist might

Massages can help relieve people's long-term pain caused by medical conditions or old injuries.

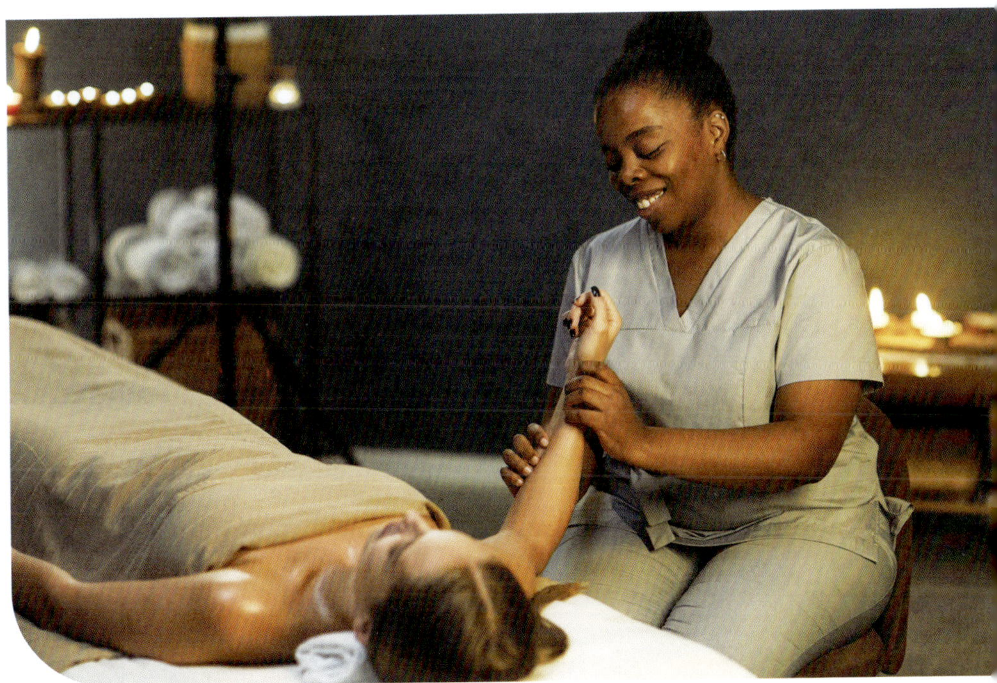

even use their forearm and elbows to do massage. A chair massage can take less than 10 minutes. But a table massage can last from 30 to 90 minutes.

The length of time and type of massage depends on the client. Massage therapist Mela Amara says:

> *There is no typical client session. Some people are coming in purely for the physical purpose of wanting the body to feel better. Some people are coming in to treat themselves.*[2]

After the session ends, therapists clean the room for the next client. They wipe down surfaces. And they put down clean blankets. Massage therapists also record any notes in their client's treatment file.

FIND OUT MORE

American Massage Therapy Association
www.amtamassage.org
The American Massage Therapy Association (AMTA) has information on massage therapist regulations for different states. AMTA also offers continuing education for massage therapists who want to improve their skills.

Massage Therapy Foundation
https://massagetherapyfoundation.org
The Massage Therapy Foundation offers many resources for therapists. These include links to scholarship opportunities and contests for students.

ESTHETICIAN

Estheticians are skin care specialists. They help clients improve the look of their skin. They also help a client's skin feel better. Estheticians use different methods. These include chemical peels. Some estheticians also do hair removal or eyelash services. Others apply permanent makeup.

Paramedical estheticians are in high demand. These specialists work with medical doctors. Experienced paramedical

Estheticians must know how to work with different skin types, such as normal, dry, and oily.

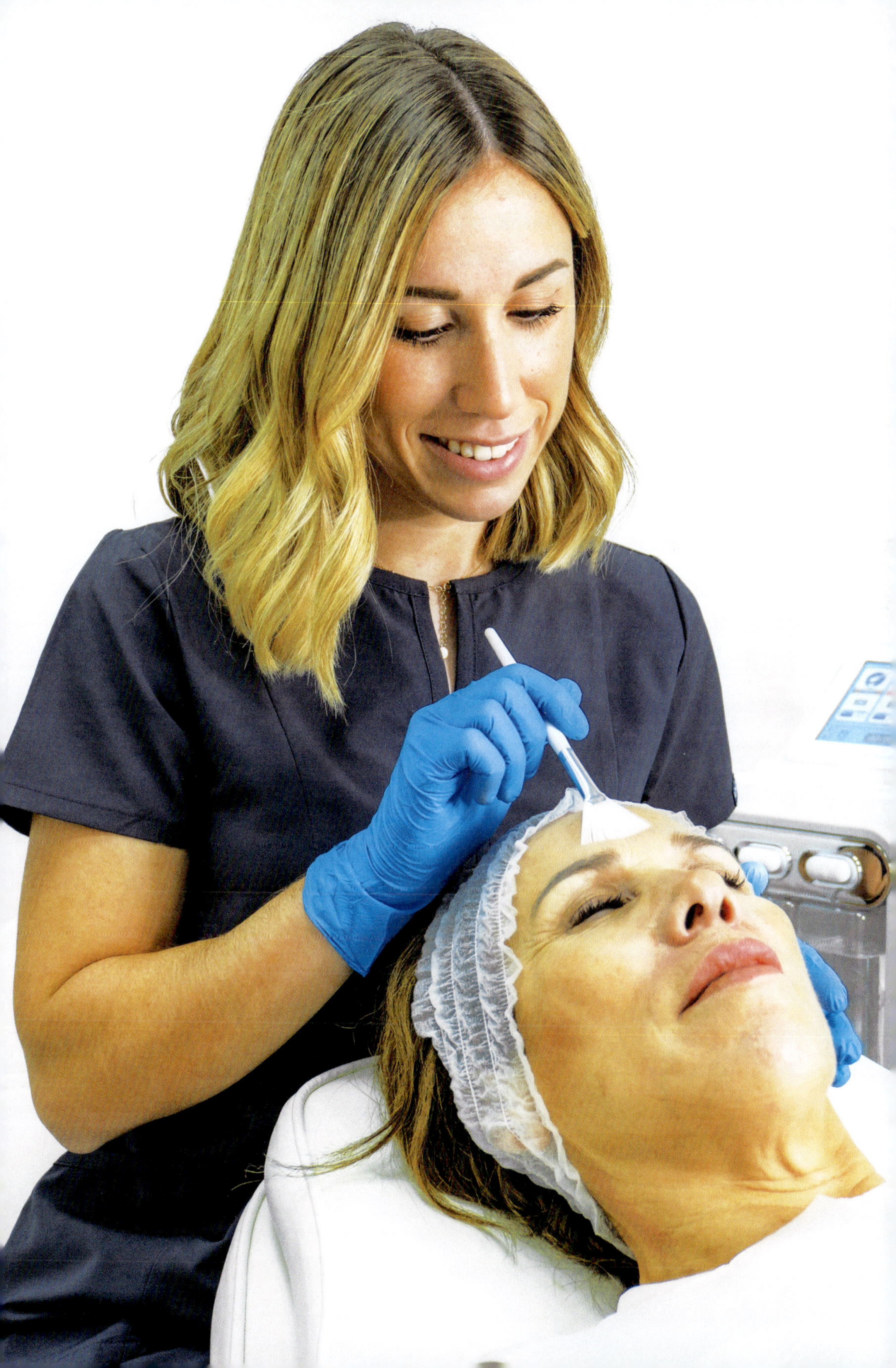

estheticians learn about **skin grafts**. They may work at burn recovery centers. Others specialize in skin conditions. These include eczema and psoriasis.

Esthetician

Minimum Education: High school diploma, vocational school
Personal Qualities: Customer-service skills, time-management skills, detail oriented
Certification and Licensing: State-approved cosmetology or esthetician license
Working Conditions: Many estheticians work in spas or salons, but some work in medical offices. They handle products with chemicals and may have to stand for long periods of time.
Average Salary: $41,560 (2024)
Number of Jobs: 81,800 (2023)
Future Job Outlook: 10 percent growth expected between 2023 and 2033

Estheticians must enjoy working with people. They must be tidy and friendly. Keeping a busy schedule requires organizational skills. The job often requires standing for long periods of time. Many estheticians are self-employed.

GETTING STARTED

Estheticians need a high school diploma. They also need a certification in **cosmetology**. Certification shows that a person has the skills and knowledge to do a job. Some high schools offer cosmetology training. But most students earn their certification at a vocational school. Programs can take between 600 and 750 hours to complete.

Some people do esthetician apprenticeships. These are training programs. They help students gain

Some estheticians get licensed as tattoo artists. This allows them to perform treatments such as microblading, which is semipermanent tattooing to make eyebrows look fuller.

hands-on experience. Students learn from professional estheticians. They also take classes to learn certain skills. Some states allow people to do an apprenticeship instead of cosmetology school.

Estheticians need a state license to work. Each state has different license requirements. Most require a certain number of training hours. Students must pass exams and a licensing test. State requirements can be found through the Associated Skin Care Professionals.

ON THE JOB

Estheticians begin by talking to clients. They discuss the goals of the client. They check the condition of the client's skin before beginning treatment.

One basic treatment is a facial. Facials clean makeup and dirt from the skin. But a facial is more than washing the face. “A facial is like a big drink of water for your skin,” says esthetician Amanda Kanaan.[3]

Skin naturally sheds dead cells. Then new cells take their place. But sometimes, dead skin cells do not fall off. This can cause dry or dark patches. Estheticians clean the skin to remove dead cells. One way to do this is by using a product

Treating Acne

Acne is a common skin condition. It happens when oil and dead skin cells clog **pores**. This can cause pimples to form on people’s skin. Estheticians are trained to treat some kinds of acne. They often use facials to help clean out pores.

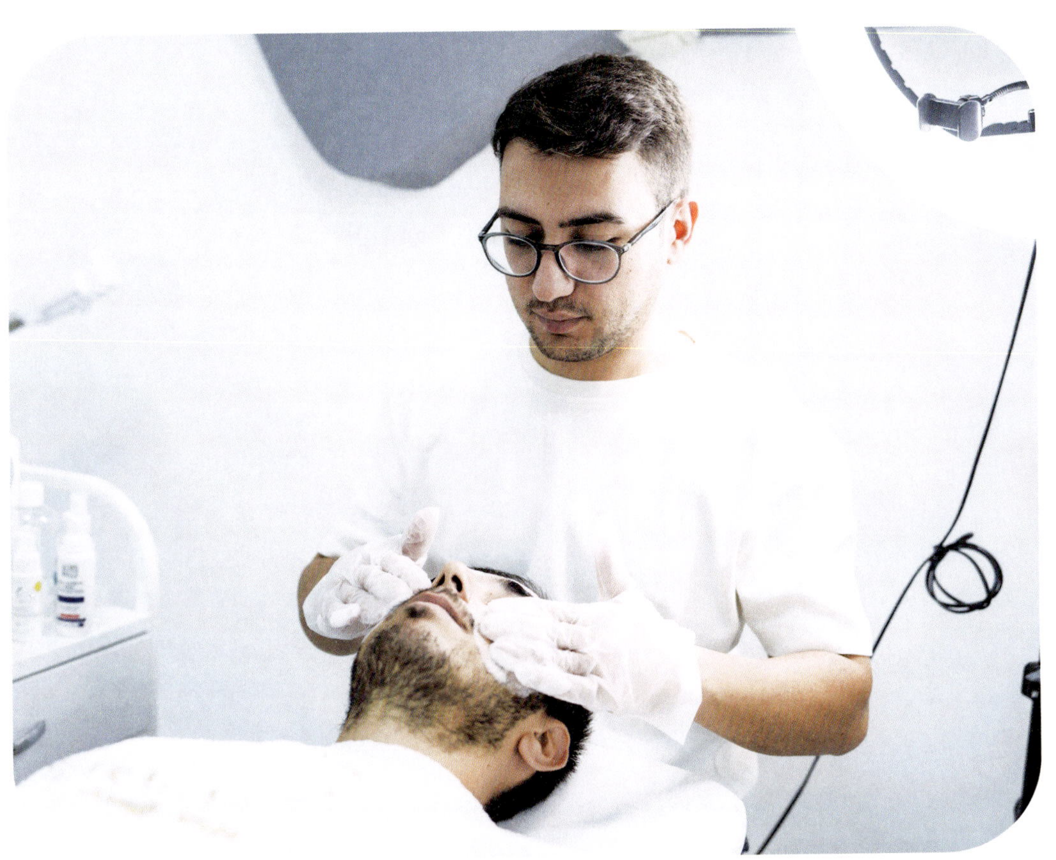

Estheticians use many kinds of masks, including clay, gel, cream, chemical, and seaweed.

with mild acid. Estheticians may use a rotating electric brush. This helps clean the face. Another method is dermaplaning. Dermaplaning is using a special blade to remove the outer layer of skin cells.

Estheticians also use masks. Masks are thick pastes. They are applied to the face.

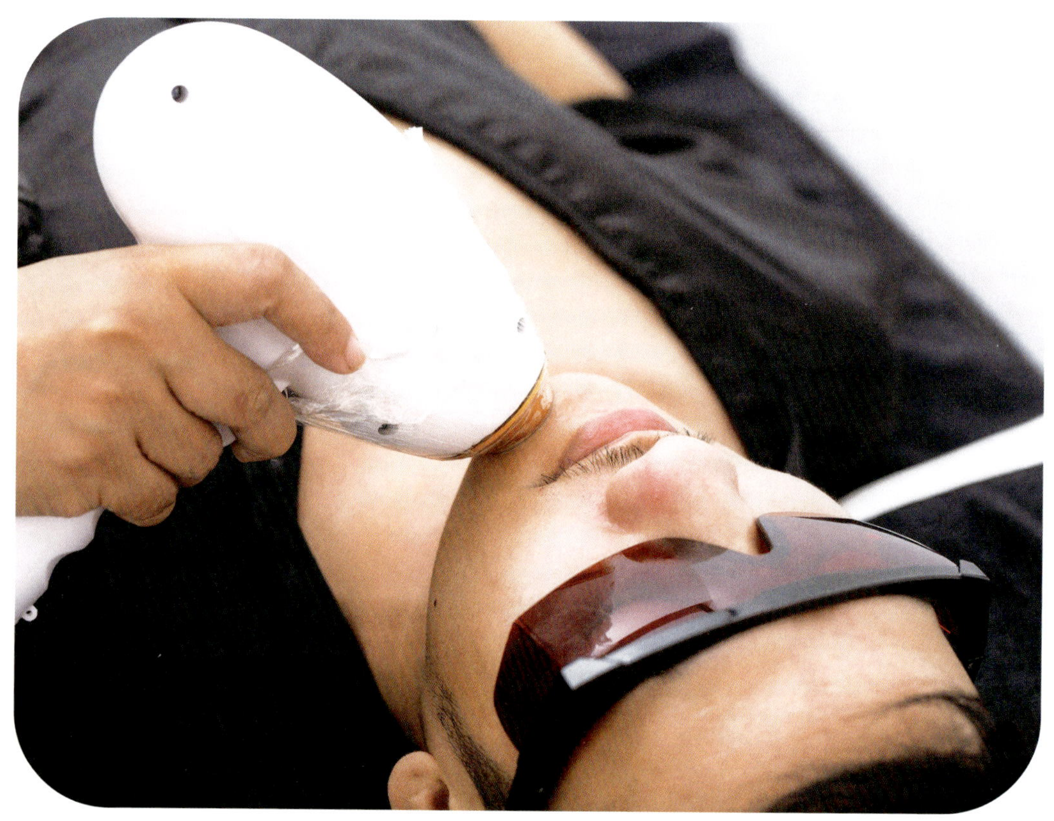

Laser hair removal usually requires between two and six sessions depending on the location of the treatment.

Each kind has a different purpose. A clay mask soaks up extra oil and cleans the skin. A mask with soy helps reduce dark spots. The facial might end with a massage and moisturizer application.

Many people pluck or shave hair from their bodies. The hair grows back quickly.

Waxing is removing hair by pulling it out instead of cutting it. Wax is spread over an area. It sticks to the hair. Then it is pulled off. Waxing keeps hair from growing back for weeks.

Some states allow estheticians to remove hair with a laser. This is a process in which a laser is aimed at a hair **follicle**. The laser heats up and damages the follicle. This causes the hair to fall out. Laser hair removal is more permanent than waxing. Some states allow only doctors to do the procedure. Others let estheticians do it while a doctor supervises.

Some estheticians specialize in lash and brow treatments. They put eyelash extensions on people. This involves gluing fibers onto natural eyelashes.

It makes eyelashes look longer and thicker. Estheticians do lash lifts, too. This procedure uses a flexible rod to curl the lashes. Lotions are applied to keep the lashes curled.

Estheticians also shape eyebrows. This is done by plucking or waxing eyebrow hairs. Cait is an esthetician. She says:

> *What I love most about being in esthetics is being able to help and inspire so many people. Whether it's helping boost someone's confidence or helping them reach their goals—being in this industry is so rewarding!*[4]

FIND OUT MORE

Associated Skin Care Professionals
www.ascpskincare.com
The Associated Skin Care Professionals (ASCP) organization has information about schools and state requirements for estheticians. ASCP also allows estheticians to connect with other people in the field.

National Coalition of Estheticians Association
https://nceacertified.org
The National Coalition of Estheticians Association (NCEA) site offers information on how people can become certified as an esthetician. NCEA also offers training programs for estheticians who want to continue their education.

CHAPTER THREE

FITNESS TRAINER

Fitness trainers lead exercise activities. There are many types of exercises. Some are for strength training. Others are for stretching. Some workouts increase blood flow for good heart health. Others help with balance. Fitness trainers motivate clients to live a healthy lifestyle.

Group fitness trainers lead people in exercise classes. Instructors often teach different types of exercise. One example

Fitness trainers ensure clients know proper lifting techniques in order to prevent injuries.

is kickboxing. Another type of fitness instructor is a personal trainer. Personal trainers work with clients one-on-one. They also work with small groups. They create training programs for people.

Fitness trainers must have good communication skills. They need to clearly

Fitness Trainer

Minimum Education: High school diploma
Personal Qualities: Good communication and social skills, physically fit
Certification and Licensing: Certification in a fitness specialty often required
Working Conditions: Fitness trainers are often on their feet. They may have to lift heavy weights or show how to do certain exercises.
Average Salary: $46,180 (2024)
Number of Jobs: 350,100 (2023)
Future Job Outlook: 14 percent growth expected between 2023 and 2033

explain exercises. They must also listen to clients' goals and needs. Trainers need to motivate clients to keep attending class. And they must show how to do exercises. Trainers often teach several classes a day. They also teach people at different fitness levels. Some clients may be professional athletes. Others may have never worked out before.

GETTING STARTED

Fitness trainers need a high school diploma. Fitness schools require a diploma to enter a certification program. Students need a certification in cardiopulmonary resuscitation (CPR). This is a procedure used if someone's heart stops beating. Many workplaces also require a certification

Fitness trainers work with people of all ages, from children to the elderly.

for using an automated external defibrillator (AED). This device gives an electrical shock to treat someone having a heart problem.

Schools offer basic fitness instructor certifications in person or online. Students learn to do exercises correctly. This helps avoid injury. They also learn about safety. Basic certification as an instructor often takes between 4 weeks and 6 months.

Certification includes a written exam. Trainers must know proper exercise techniques. They should know how to assess a client's fitness level. This helps trainers create a proper fitness routine. Certification may also require a video or live demonstration of skills.

Personal trainers need a different certification. The American Council on Exercise offers certifications. Personal trainers determine a client's health and goals. Then they develop an exercise program based on that information. Personal trainers must learn to adjust exercises for people with health problems. And they must keep track of a person's progress.

ON THE JOB

Some fitness trainers work in private or public fitness centers. Others hold classes in parks. Personal trainers sometimes work in clients' homes. Or they may have their own gym. Some coach online. Many fitness trainers work at more than one facility. They may teach a class two nights at one place. Then they do personal training in the mornings at another. Fitness trainers may have several jobs.

Group trainers develop an exercise routine for a class. They might select music that goes with the movements. Some specialize in classes for children or seniors. Others teach exercise routines created by fitness companies. Companies often certify instructors to teach their workouts.

Group classes sometimes use equipment. This includes weights. After class, trainers make sure equipment is cleaned.

One benefit of being a fitness trainer is having a flexible schedule. This gives trainers time to take care of personal responsibilities. But it does not mean working only when someone feels like it. Pete McCall is a fitness trainer and blogger.

Online Fitness Coach

An online fitness coach teaches fitness on a website or phone app. They create content such as videos. They help people do exercises from home. Some online coaches have virtual classes. Others may develop workouts for individuals. Online coaches can work from anywhere. They must know how to promote themselves to keep clients coming back.

He advises that trainers have to work when clients want to work out. He says:

> *To be successful and ensure a financially [profitable] career, personal trainers need to decide when they want to work to meet the demands of the local market and should plan on being available at those times.*[5]

Another benefit of fitness training is being self-employed. In 2023, about 16 percent of trainers were self-employed. Many love the job because it allows them to keep up their own fitness while helping others. Claudia Amy Salador is a trainer. She says, “As a [personal trainer], work and exercise are one and the same.”[6] Fitness trainers enjoy helping others live healthy lifestyles.

FIND OUT MORE

American Council on Exercise

www.acefitness.org

The American Council on Exercise (ACE) offers certifications for all levels of fitness instructors. It also has resources to help people build a career as a fitness professional.

National Academy of Sports Medicine

www.nasm.org

The National Academy of Sports Medicine (NASM) offers personal trainer certification in various areas of fitness and wellness training. These include certification in nutrition and sports performance.

CHAPTER FOUR

HAIRSTYLIST OR BARBER

Hairstylists and barbers are specialists in hair care. They check a person's scalp and hair. They recommend treatments for dry or oily hair. Stylists discuss hairstyle options with clients. They can change hair color. They can chemically change the texture. Stylists also cut and style hair.

Barbers specialize in hair care for men. They cut and style hair, too. But they also cut or trim facial hair. Barbers may

The four major hair types that hairstylists and barbers work with are straight, wavy, curly, and coily.

fit hairpieces. In some states, they can also color hair.

Stylists and barbers must have good customer-service skills. This makes

Hairstylist or Barber

Minimum Education: High school diploma, vocational school

Personal Qualities: Good customer and time-management skills, creativity, tidiness

Certification and Licensing: Certificate in cosmetology and state licensing

Working Conditions: Hairstylists and barbers often stand for long periods of time. They also work with chemicals that are found in hair products.

Average Salary: $35,420 (2024)

Number of Jobs: 649,400 (2023)

Future Job Outlook: 7 percent growth expected between 2023 and 2033

customers want to come back. The job requires long hours of standing. The work area must be kept clean and tidy. Hair appointments take different amounts of time. This means staying organized and keeping on schedule.

GETTING STARTED

Hairstylists and barbers often need a high school diploma. Hairstylists must attend a cosmetology program. States require an average of 1,500 hours of instruction. This can take 9 to 12 months. Programs teach how to use chemicals and styling tools safely. They stress **hygiene** to avoid spreading diseases. Students learn about hairstyling. Cosmetology programs also teach the basics of makeup and skin care.

Washing a client's hair helps get rid of any oil or product buildup and provides a clean surface for hair professionals to work with.

Barbers attend a barber program. These programs usually take about 9 months. They offer classroom study and hands-on training. Barbers learn proper hygiene. They also learn about scalp diseases. Students are taught how to use a straight razor for shaving. This includes learning how to take care of the blade.

States require all hair care professionals to have a license to work. Each state has different requirements. Most require proof of graduating from a state-approved program. Students then take a written exam. Some states require a skills demonstration. This means students must prove their skills to be licensed.

New barbers often begin working for an experienced barber. Many work on commission. This means they split the money for a haircut. Typically, 60 percent of the money goes to the barber. The other 40 percent goes to the shop. As new barbers gain clients, they may rent a barber chair at the shop. This helps them earn more money. Some barbers have their own shops.

Hair professionals do more training over time. They need to keep up with new techniques and styles. Some states require stylists to continue taking classes. Hair care professionals may also take classes in managing a business.

ON THE JOB

Hairstylists and barbers spend most of their day working with clients. They must be friendly and enjoy working with people. A big part of their success is connecting with clients. Between clients, stylists and barbers clean their work area and equipment. They restock supplies. At the end of the day, they check the next day's schedule.

Hair care professionals have flexible hours. They can choose to work part-time

Hairstylist and barber students often use wigs to practice different cutting, styling, and coloring techniques.

or full-time. They may schedule around personal responsibilities. Some might prefer working in the morning. Others might work only in the evenings.

Many hair professionals enjoy the artistic and creative part of hairstyling. Megan Weese is a stylist. She says, "Each client is a unique canvas, allowing me to experiment

Hairstylists and barbers use a variety of tools and devices, such as scissors, hair clippers, curling irons, and blow-dryers.

with different styles, colors, and techniques to enhance their natural beauty."[7]

About 48 percent of hairstylists are self-employed. And 80 percent of barbers are self-employed. Some hair professionals own their own shops. But many rent spaces in spas or hair salons.

Many hairstylists have a specialty. One example is textured-hair specialists. They work with curly or kinky hair. They train to use the best products and techniques for these hair types. Some stylists work in film or TV. They may have to re-create historical hairstyles. They might also need to know how to work with wigs.

African Braiding Specialist

African braiding specialists offer braiding services. These are often for Black clients. African braiding uses a technique that braids hair close to the scalp. This creates raised rows of hair. Decorative beads can be woven into the braids. Braiders might also add extensions. These are pieces of fake or natural hair that make people's real hair longer.

Drew Danburry opened his own shop after finishing barber school. He offers haircuts and straight razor shaves. Danburry says, "I cut hair and make people look just the way they want, and I get to meet new people all the time. It's fun, creative, and I like feeling satisfied with my work."[8]

When working with chemicals or using hair dyes, stylists should wear gloves to protect their skin.

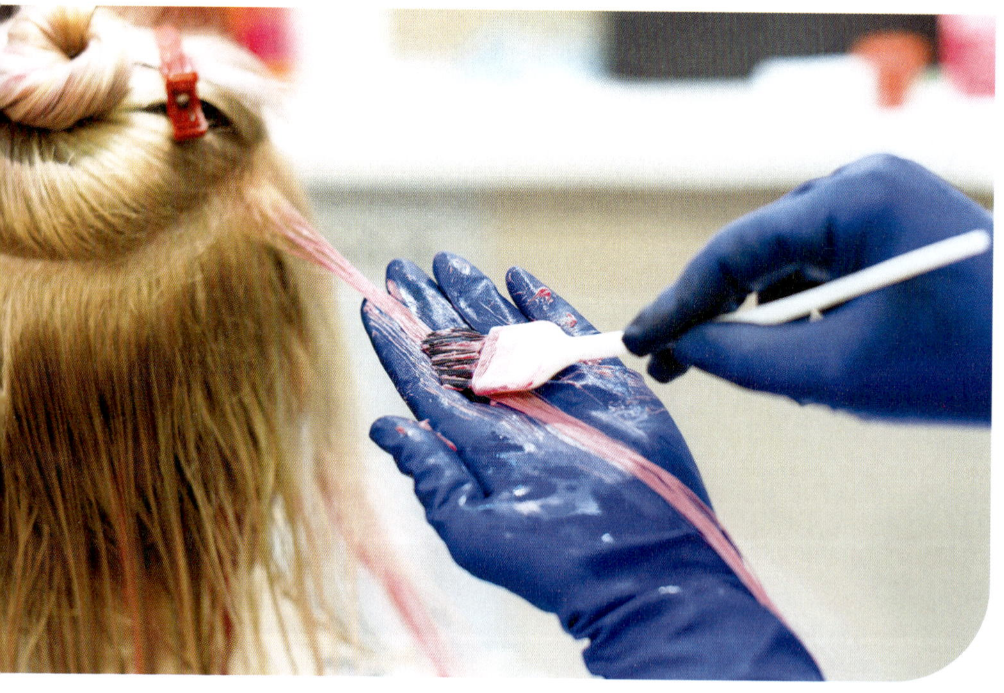

FIND OUT MORE

American Barber Association
https://americanbarber.org
The American Barber Association (ABA) is an organization that provides information on the standards in barber care. The ABA site includes certifications and educational programs for both students and professionals.

Associated Hair Professionals
www.associatedhairprofessionals.com
The Associated Hair Professionals website offers resources for students and professionals in the hairstyling industry. This includes a Cosmetology Schools directory for people to search for beauty schools near them.

OTHER JOBS IN THE WELLNESS AND BEAUTY INDUSTRY

Manicurist and Pedicurist

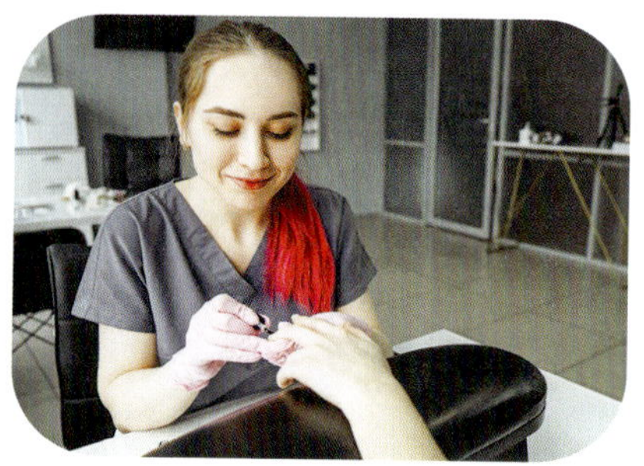

Manicurists take care of fingernails. Pedicurists take care of toenails. Both are sometimes called nail technicians. Nail technicians clean, trim, and file nails. They often begin treatment by soaking the client's nails. Then they remove artificial nails and rough skin. During a treatment, they massage and moisturize hands or feet. Manicurists and pedicurists add nail polish or create nail art. They also put on fake nails.

Makeup Artist

Makeup artists apply makeup on people's faces or bodies. Some work in salons or spas. Others work in film, television, or fashion. Customers may hire makeup artists for weddings or other special occasions. Artists can change a customer's look based on an event. Special effects artists may change an actor's appearance by adding scars or making them look older. They might also create alien characters or monsters.

Yoga Instructor

Yoga is an ancient practice used to increase wellness. Yoga instructors guide students in different yoga poses and movements. This increases strength and flexibility. Instructors also teach breathing techniques and meditation. This improves mental wellness. There are many types of yoga. Some feature gentle exercises. Others have more difficult moves. Instructors might teach various types of yoga. They also teach people of all ages.

Aromatherapist

Aromatherapists use essential oils to improve wellness. Essential oils are liquids that often smell nice. Aromatherapists rub the oils into people's skin. Or they may use a device that releases the oil into the air. The smells encourage the brain to release natural chemicals. These affect moods and emotions. Aromatherapy also relaxes muscles and improves sleep. Therapists are trained to use the right oil and the proper amount to ease symptoms.

GLOSSARY

anatomy

the study of the parts of the human body

cadavers

dead human bodies, often used by medical students or professionals for study

cosmetology

the study and application of beauty treatments for the hair, skin, and nails

follicle

a structure in people's skin from which hair grows

hygiene

cleanliness practices to remain healthy and prevent diseases

manipulate

using the hands to move or apply force to soft tissues

pores

tiny openings in the skin that release oil and sweat

rehabilitation

restoring to health using training or therapy

skin grafts

pieces of healthy skin that are surgically placed on a damaged area of a person's body

SOURCE NOTES

CHAPTER ONE: MASSAGE THERAPIST

1. Cindy Williams, "Benefits of Being a Massage Therapist," *Associated Bodywork & Massage Professionals,* March 17, 2023. www.abmp.com.

2. Quoted in Kit Harlow, "A Day in the Life of a Massage Therapist," *Northwestern University Health Sciences*, n.d. www.nwhealth.edu.

CHAPTER TWO: ESTHETICIAN

3. Quoted in "Facials: What Are They, and What Do They Really Do?" *Cleveland Clinic*, August 28, 2023. https://health.clevelandclinic.org.

4. Quoted in Samantha Reed and Courtney Adema, "Six Estheticians on Why They Love Their Careers," *American Spa*, October 15, 2019. www.americanspa.com.

CHAPTER THREE: FITNESS TRAINER

5. Pete McCall, "Typical Day in the Life of an NASM Personal Trainer," *NASM*, n.d. https://blog.nasm.org.

6. Claudia Amy Salador, "Ten Reasons Why I Became a Personal Trainer," *Medium*, September 11, 2018. https://medium.com.

CHAPTER FOUR: HAIRSTYLIST OR BARBER

7. Quoted in "'I Am a Hairstylist, Because . . .'" *Salon Services Pro*, April 29, 2024. www.salonservicespro.com.

8. Quoted in Brett and Kate McKay, "So You Want My Job: Barber," *Art of Manliness*, September 25, 2021. www.artofmanliness.com.

INDEX

IMAGE CREDITS

Cover: © Rawpixel.com/Shutterstock Images
4: Red Line Editorial
5: Red Line Editorial
7: © Hananeko_Studio/Shutterstock Images
8: © Marko Poplasen/Shutterstock Images
11: © santypan/Shutterstock Images
13: © Shakirov Albert/Shutterstock Images
16: © Aya Images/Shutterstock Images
19: © Dragon Images/Shutterstock Images
21: © Dragon Images/Shutterstock Images
25: © Manu Pousa/Shutterstock Images
28: © hedgehog94/Shutterstock Images
31: © ZeynepKaya/iStockphoto
32: © MDV Edwards/Shutterstock Images
37: © Papalah/Shutterstock Images
40: © Baza Production/Shutterstock Images
47: © LightField Studios/Shutterstock Images
50: © Nikodash/Shutterstock Images
53: © Asia-Pacific Images Studio/iStockphoto
54: © Guillermo Spelucin R./Shutterstock Images
56: © IMG Stock Studio/Shutterstock Images
58 (top): © Tatiana Maksimova/Shutterstock Images
58 (bottom): © Africa Studio/Shutterstock Images
59 (top): © Zdenka Darula/Shutterstock Images
59 (bottom): © polinaloves/Shutterstock Images

ABOUT THE AUTHOR

Cynthia Kennedy Henzel has degrees in education and geography. She has written more than a hundred books for young people. These include fiction and nonfiction on subjects such as geography, science, culture, and history. Henzel enjoys discovering new things—especially the many career opportunities she never knew about. She highly recommends keeping fit and using sunscreen.